My Runaway Shadow!

Written by Merle Pyke
Illustrations by Stacey Johnson

My Runaway Shadow

Dedication:

This book is lovingly dedicated to my grandsons—Declan, Bransen, Grayson, Lochlan—and my dear friend Donna Mikla, as well as to all the inquisitive, adventurous, and slightly mischievous children who constantly ask 'why?'. It is meant for those who bravely confront the uncertainties of a new school, welcome new challenges, or cultivate budding friendships. It is for the dreamers who imagine castles in the sky and find magic in the ordinary. Additionally, this story is dedicated to Gladstone Public School, where my father, my four sons, and I all received our elementary education. I will forever cherish the memory of Mrs. Joanne Hunter, the teacher who had the greatest impact on my life.

My Runaway Shadow

Declan clutched his backpack, the soft material feeling strangely cold against his sweaty palms as he swung it to his back. Gladstone Public School or Happy Rock, as his dad and his uncles use to call it, loomed before him, a brick giant buzzing with the excited chatter of children. He felt a familiar knot tighten in his stomach – the first-day jitters. He'd moved so many times, each new school a fresh wave of anxieties. Would he make friends? Would he get lost? Would the teachers be nice? He took a deep breath, reminding himself of his mom's words: "Be brave, Declan. New beginnings are always exciting."

Just as he felt the weight of his nervousness beginning to overwhelm him, a bright voice resonated throughout the playground, "Hey, welcome, Declan, to Gladstone Public School!" exclaimed Mrs. Mikla, his new teacher. Her words, filled with contagious enthusiasm, acted like a comforting breeze, dispelling his anxieties.

My Runaway Shadow

The schoolyard, bathed in the golden light of an autumn morning, was a vibrant explosion of colour. Crimson and gold leaves crunched underfoot, a symphony of rustles accompanying the joyous squeals of children. Declan's eyes were immediately drawn to a magnificent oak tree, its branches reaching towards the sky like outstretched arms. A swing set, painted in cheerful colours, swayed gently in the breeze, inviting him to join the fun.

SCHOOL **BELL**

When suddenly without warning, the school bell sounded, prompting all the students to form a line and prepare to enter the school. "Class, please line up here." said Mrs. Mikla.

The students proceeded through the door of their classroom. Each desk was labeled with a name, indicating where each student should sit. Declan swiftly located his name and took a seat. Although he felt a bit anxious, the fact that Mrs. Mikla was his teacher brought him some comfort.

"Students," Mrs. Mikla instructed, "please take out your pencils and write your name at the top of the paper." The assignment was titled "Wilderness Wednesday - All About Clouds." Declan promptly retrieved his pencil and wrote his name on the paper.

Mrs. Mikla, with a smile as bright as the sun, was everything Declan had hoped for and more. She had kind eyes that crinkled at the corners when she laughed, and a voice that was both gentle and authoritative. "Today, we're cloud detectives!" she announced, her voice ringing with excitement. "We're going on a cloud-spotting adventure just before recess! Let's start with learning about all the different types of clouds that we may see on our exploration. There are cumulus clouds, cirrus clouds, and stratus clouds. First, we will talk about my favourite clouds called the cumulus clouds!"

She pointed to her drawing on the board of a fluffy, white cloud. "These are like giant cotton balls," she explained, her voice light and engaging. "They're puffy and white and often look like popcorn scattered across the sky. They're usually a sign of fair weather."

Declan found himself nodding along, his earlier anxieties melting away with the lightness of her words. He'd always loved looking at clouds, but he'd never known there were so many different types.

Mrs. Mikla then instructed all the students to use their pencils to draw a picture of cumulus clouds and to label them accordingly. She pointed to the board for the correct spelling of the term "cumulus." Mrs. Mikla continued on, "Please signal with a thumbs up once you have finished drawing your clouds."

Declan immediately began his task of illustrating a cumulus cloud. He inscribed the phrase "Cumulus Clouds" and connected it to the drawing with a line.

Then, Mrs. Mikla moved onto cirrus clouds, drawing a picture of wispy, feathery formations. "These are high-flying clouds, made of tiny ice crystals," she explained. "They're often thin and wispy, like strokes of a painter's brush across the sky. See how delicate they look? Sometimes they look like little feathery horses galloping across the sky!"

Declan chuckled to himself as he envisioned the fluffy white horses dashing across the blue sky. Each horse moved swiftly, their gallops filled with elegance and poise. Declan had a profound affection for horses, which sparked his vivid imagination.

And once again, Mrs. Mikla instructed all the students to use their pencils to illustrate their own cirrus clouds and provide an appropriate label for their drawing.

Mrs. Mikla announced to the students, "Ok. Now, I will give you about three minutes to finish this up. Once done, please signal with a thumbs up that you have finished your drawing of your cirrus clouds."

Declan immediately began sketching his cirrus cloud. He inscribed the phrase "Cirrus Clouds" and connected it to the illustration with a wavy line.

Finally, Mrs. Mikla then introduced stratus clouds, describing them as flat, grey layers that covered the sky like a blanket. "These often bring drizzle or light rain," she explained, "but they can also be quite beautiful in their own way. Imagine them as giant, soft blankets, snuggling the Earth." She encouraged the children to share their own observations, their imaginative descriptions adding another layer of wonder to the lesson.

The students engaged in a lighthearted conversation with their peers about the amusing shapes and creative figures they observed in stratus clouds. Mrs. Mikla reminded them, with a chuckle, not to forget to

My Runaway Shadow

label the stratus clouds themselves, rather than the whimsical images they imagined seeing.

As Declan listened, he felt a sense of belonging wash over him. He was no longer the nervous new boy; he was a cloud detective, embarking on an exciting adventure. He glanced around and spotted a boy with bright, curious eyes and a mop of unruly brown hair. The boy was staring intently out the window at a particularly fluffy cumulus cloud, a wide grin spread across his face.

"Wow, look at that cumulus cloud!" the boy exclaimed, pointing towards a magnificent cloud formation that resembled a sheep. "It looks like a fluffy cotton candy sheep! Yummy."

My Runaway Shadow

Declan smiled. "It sure does," he agreed, feeling a sudden surge of warmth and connection. "I'm Declan."

"I'm Bransen," the boy replied, extending a hand. "Those are pretty awesome clouds, huh?"

Declan nodded enthusiastically. "They certainly are! I never knew there were so many different types of clouds. I always thought clouds were just - clouds," They shared a laugh together.

As they waited for the other students to catch up, Declan and Bransen spent the rest of the lesson comparing notes, pointing out different cloud formations in books and sharing their imaginative interpretations. They discovered a shared passion for the wonders of the sky, a common ground that instantly bonded them.

Mrs. Mikla addressed the students, announcing that it was time for their picture walk. She encouraged them to stand and observe their classmates' artwork, specifically the various artistic representations of each of the different clouds that each student had created.

The students rose from their seats and moved about the classroom, observing the artwork created by their peers. Each student had a unique interpretation of the appearance of clouds. Some students remarked that one particular cloud resembled a train.

Mrs. Mikla remarked that it appears we have all completed our picture walk. Mrs. Mikla then clapped her hands three times and then instructed, "One, two, three, eyes on me." In response, the class echoed, "One, two, eyes on you," directing their attention to Mrs. Mikla.

"Now that I have your attention," Mrs. Mikla announced to the class, "it is time to head outside to explore the playground and engage in our cloud observation." She noted that the sun was about to emerge, which would certainly enhance their outdoor experience of observing the clouds. She instructed everyone to line up at the door and prepare for the outing.

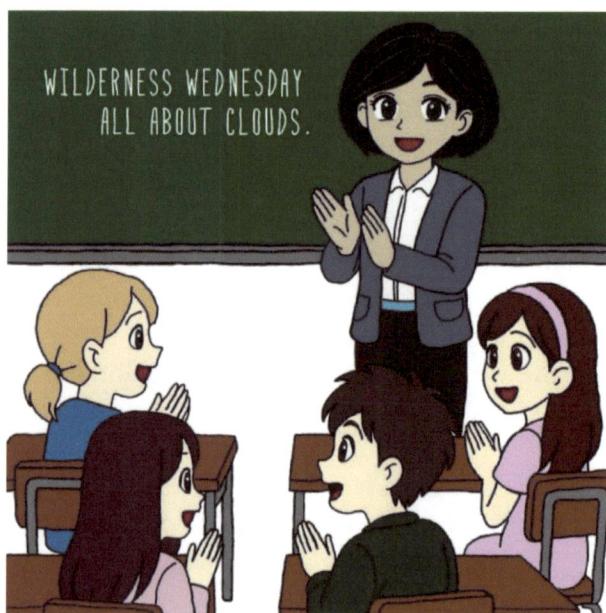

Today marked Wilderness Wednesday, a day dedicated to learning about the environment and ways to protect it. The students promptly stood up and formed an orderly line at the door. Declan and Bransen ensured they were partners for Wilderness Wednesday, with Bransen explaining that every Wednesday, they have the opportunity to learn outdoors.

After a short walk, the students reached the playground. "Remain with your partners," instructed Mrs. Mikla. "Students, spread out and direct your gaze towards the sky. What kind of clouds do you see?" Declan raised his hand and responded, "Those are cumulus clouds."

"You are correct, Declan," Mrs. Mikla acknowledged. "And here comes our gorgeous sun," she added. "Look! Can everyone see their shadow?" she inquired. The students began to dance around, delighting in how their shadows mirrored their every movement.

My Runaway Shadow

Suddenly, as Declan was describing a cumulus cloud that resembled a mischievous monkey, when he noticed something peculiar. His shadow! It seemed to have a life of its own. It wasn't just a dark imprint following his movements; it was dancing, prancing, and even seemed to be mimicking his expressions. He looked down, startled. His shadow had actually lifted a few centimetres off the ground, as if performing a little hop!

Bransen, noticing Declan's surprise, burst out laughing. "Your shadow is breakdancing!" he exclaimed. "It's super cool, eh?"

My Runaway Shadow

Declan chuckled, caught between amusement and astonishment. This was far from an ordinary shadow; it was a whimsical and playful entity, eager for its own escapade. Then, like a flash, the sun just vanished, consumed by the cumulus clouds. At that moment, everyone's shadows faded away. Everyone's except for Declan's.

The shadow, emboldened by its newfound independence, began a playful chase across the playground. It darted between the legs of other children, dodged the swings with surprising agility, and even attempted a daring climb up a nearby tree.

My Runaway Shadow

"Declan, where are you headed?" Mrs. Mikla called out. Bransen responded, "It's Declan's shadow. It seems to have a mind of its own and is trying to escape from him." "What? Really?" exclaimed Mrs. Mikla, her eyes widening in astonishment. She turned to see Declan's shadow indeed fleeing from him.

The chase became a schoolyard spectacle. Other children, initially surprised, quickly joined in the fun, adding to the joyful chaos. Laughter echoed through the playground as Declan and Bransen pursued the rogue shadow, their yells and squeals blending with the autumn breeze.

The vibrant colours of the playground – the bright yellow swing, the red and blue slides, the deep green grass – formed a lively backdrop to their comical pursuit. The shadow, ever elusive, seemed to delight in leading them on, its movements growing increasingly erratic and unpredictable.

My Runaway Shadow

The sun began to emerge once more from behind the fluffy cumulus clouds, casting its light upon the playground. All the students began to observe their shadows once again. Declan looked down. "Where has my shadow gone?" inquired Declan. He discovered that his shadow was concealed within that of another student, hiding as if to avoid detection.

"There it is!" exclaimed Bransen. In an attempt to capture his elusive shadow, Declan performed a clumsy ``Elmer`` ninja roll on the ground, prompting laughter and excitement from Bransen and his classmates.

My Runaway Shadow

However, the shadow appeared to be just playing games with Declan and Bransen, evading capture with a relentless determination, particularly from Declan. Like his father, Declan was an agile runner and had nearly succeeded in catching the shadow on several occasions. If only I could grasp it, I could force it to remain as my shadow instead of fleeing,

Declan contemplated. "Bransen," Declan called out, "you head in that direction while I go this way. Together, we should be able to trap my shadow." The two boys quickly formulated a plan and chased after the elusive shadow. Mrs. Mikla was starting to grow increasingly impatient with both the boys and Declan's runaway shadow.

My Runaway Shadow

'You need to capture it - promptly; our snack time at school is approaching,' Mrs. Mikla insisted. 'Bransen, please accompany Declan and attempt to retrieve that crazy shadow.' 'Certainly, Mrs. Mikla,' replied Bransen. 'However, do not venture beyond the schoolyard,' Mrs. Mikla cautioned. Bransen then hurriedly dashed after Declan.

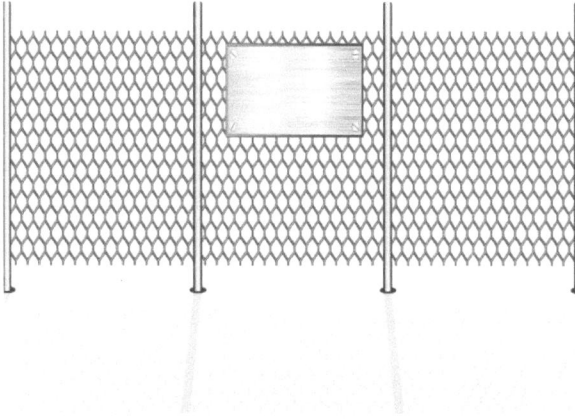

The pursuit did not conclude at the boundary of the playground. Instead, the shadow guided them on an exhilarating adventure into the adjacent park. 'Wait,' Bransen interjected, 'we are not permitted to leave the school grounds.' 'But I have to. I must find my shadow,' Declan insisted.

This park, a captivating green area that bordered the school, presented an intriguing new landscape. Majestic oak trees loomed overhead, casting elongated

My Runaway Shadow

shadows, their foliage transitioning into hues of burnt orange and deep crimson.

Vividly coloured flowers adorned the grassy mounds, their petals strikingly bright against the dark soil. It was an ideal location for a shadow to conceal itself. The boys paused and surveyed their surroundings in search of Declan's shadow.

The shadow, however, proved to be a remarkably agile opponent. It scampered up trees with astonishing ease, its dark form a fleeting silhouette against the dappled sunlight filtering through the leaves. It teased squirrels, causing them to chatter indignantly from their high perches. It even appeared to momentarily blend in with the shadows cast by the trees, momentarily disappearing only to reappear at unexpected locations, further adding to the excitement of the chase.

My Runaway Shadow

As the sun began to dip behind the cumulus clouds, Declan and Bransen, exhausted but undeterred, paused beneath a majestic oak tree. They were out of breath, their clothes slightly rumpled, but their spirits still remained high. The playful chase had been exhilarating, but they were determined to catch this runaway shadow.

"We need a different plan," Bransen stated decisively, his eyes shining with determination. Declan, reflecting on Mrs. Mikla's cloud lesson, realized that his shadow seemed to react to light and movement.

The sun once more vanished behind the cumulus clouds, providing Declan and Bransen with even more respite. This gave him an idea. A clever, slightly mischievous idea, mirroring the shadow's own antics. He grinned at Bransen. "I think I've got it."

My Runaway Shadow

``But we have to be patient. As soon as the sun re-appears, follow my lead, `` Declan instructed. Declan's shadow, once a mere appendage, now possessed a mischievous glint, a playful defiance in its every hop and skip.

The shadow observed Declan and Bransen, pondering their activities. Was the game concluded, the shadow wondered. "Are you ready? Follow me," Declan encouraged as the sun started to emerge from behind the clouds. The shadow, which had appeared from behind the oak tree, seemed confused, yet it began to follow the boys back to the school playground. Declan noted, "It's working; my shadow is following us."

In the distance, the boys could hear the sound of the recess bell ringing. 'It is time for recess,' Bransen announced. 'We should quickly return to the school.' He added that with all the students outside for recess, Declan's shadow would have numerous places to conceal itself.

SCHOOL BELL

'Yes, indeed,' Declan concurred. With that, they hurried back to the schoolyard.

My Runaway Shadow

The shadow, a nimble acrobat in the mid-morning sun, was surprisingly quick. It did run back to the school playground. It weaved through the legs of children playing hopscotch, dodged the swirling skirts of girls playing jump rope, and even managed a daring leap over a low-lying fence, its dark form a blur against the vibrant colours of the playground. The bright red of the swings, the sunny yellow of the slide, and the deep green of the grass formed a vivid backdrop to the chase, a kaleidoscope of colours contrasting with the playful darkness of the runaway shadow.

The shadow was resolute in its decision to prolong the game of evasion from Declan. It employed various tactics to lure the boys into pursuing it once more. But the shadow was beginning to get tired from all that running, climbing, and dodging the boys.

Declan then observed his shadow resting against the fence, it looked like his shadow was breathing heavily and he thought to himself – this is my chance to reclaim it. He decided to move to the right while signaling for Bransen to take the left path, both determined to retrieve the elusive shadow. Suddenly, the sun reappeared, illuminating the playground and enabling all the students outside during recess to see their own shadows. In that instant, Declan came to the realization that his shadow had disappeared once more.

Bransen began to express his fatigue, noting that recess was nearing its end. Declan acknowledged this, stating that assistance was necessary. He then called out

My Runaway Shadow

to the other students on the playground, saying, "Hey everyone! My shadow isn't acting like a proper shadow. Can you help me catch it?" The students responded with enthusiasm, turning their attention to the ground in search of the elusive shadow.

The other children, initially spectators, now actively participated, their cheers and laughter adding to the festive atmosphere. They pointed and giggled, their eyes wide with wonder and amusement. Some tried to help Declan and Bransen, their small hands outstretched, attempting to capture the shadow as it darted past. It was a communal effort, a shared experience that transcended the usual divisions of playground games. The shadow, in its unexpected rebellion, had brought the entire schoolyard together, united in a moment of shared amusement and wonder.

The shadow was pleased to see that the game had resumed, with all the students were participating this time. They pursued the shadow throughout the playground, while the shadow skillfully evaded capture by weaving in and out. Until...

Lochlan screamed out, "I will catch it," as he sprinted across the playground, pursued by his fellow students.

Grayson yelled, "I got it, I got your shadow," as he grasped the leg of Declan's shadow. When suddenly, the shadow broke free from Grayson's hold. And dashed off again.

The shadow, finally seeming to tire, perched briefly atop a low-hanging branch, its dark form a tiny silhouette against the fiery sun. For a moment, a sense of quiet contemplation settled over the group of children, the energy of the chase replaced by a shared moment of awe.

Declan, recalling Mrs. Mikla's lesson on the unpredictable nature of clouds, remembered how their shapes shifted and changed, mirroring the ever-changing landscape of the sky. He realized that his shadow, in its playful defiance, might be mirroring his own inner energy,

My Runaway Shadow

his own capacity for spontaneous joy and adventure. This realization deepened his understanding not just of his shadow but of himself.

Declan and Bransen heard the recess bell ring, signaling that it was time for students to return indoors. As Declan's shadow became visible, everyone resumed their way back to school, oblivious to its presence. The shadow attempted once more to leap in front of Declan and Bransen to capture their attention, as it was not finished with its playful antics.

SCHOOL **BELL**

The two boys exchanged glances just before seizing and grabbing the shadow. Declan declared, "I've got you now. There's no way for you to escape." The shadow merely trailed behind the boys as they entered the school.

As the sun set, the shadow vanished. "Wait," Declan thought, stepping back outside in front of the sun. The shadow reemerged. "Excellent, this is your rightful place," Declan remarked. The shadow gave him a thumbs up. And Declan returned to his class.

Once in the classroom, Declan and Bransen asked Mrs. Mikla, "What's the theme for next week's Wilderness

Wednesday?" Mrs. Mikla replied, "It's all about trees." Bransen then wondered, "Can anything go wrong with trees?" Declan chimed in, "I really hope not!" They both chuckled, thinking about how memorable this Wilderness Wednesday had been.

Declan remarked that the focus should have been on his shadow rather than on clouds. Bransen concurred, stating that they dedicated more time pursuing Declan's shadow than searching for clouds. However, next Wednesday will be centered around trees, which cannot escape. Or can they? Both boys chuckled.

"Class, please take out your writing materials, we are going to write in our journals today about what happened during your recess," Mrs. Mikla instructed.

The End.

My Runaway Shadow

Appendix:

This appendix includes some helpful cloud identification tips to help you on your own cloud-spotting adventures! Remember to always observe clouds safely and with adult supervision.

Identifying Cumulus Clouds:

These puffy, cotton-ball-like clouds are often associated with fair weather. They are typically white or light gray, with flat bases and rounded tops.

Cumulus Clouds

Identifying Cirrus Clouds:

These wispy, feathery clouds are high in the atmosphere and are made of ice crystals. They often appear as delicate strands or streaks across the sky.

Cirrus Clouds

My Runaway Shadow

Identifying Stratus Clouds:

These low-lying, layered clouds are often associated with overcast skies and light rain or drizzle. They appear as a gray sheet covering the sky.

Stratus Clouds

My Runaway Shadow

Author Biography

Merle Pyke is an enthusiastic storyteller who has cherished a deep-seated passion for fantasy and adventure throughout his life. He is continually fascinated by the transformative power of imagination and the enchantment of narrative. He holds the conviction that stories have the ability to whisk readers away to different realms, impart important lessons, and spark creativity. Outside of his writing endeavors, Merle Pyke loves to spend quality time with his family and dogs, and he relishes a fine cup of coffee.

https://www.amazon.ca/s?k=merle+pyke

https://books.by/pyke-books-publishing

My Runaway Shadow

Illustrator Biography:

Stacey Johnson is a dedicated illustrator who has a deep passion for digital art and sketching. Her artistic journey commenced in her childhood, and throughout the years, she has refined her abilities to convey emotions, narratives, and vivid imagery through her creations. Outside of her drawing endeavors, Stacey cherishes moments with her husband and children, and she loves to doodle on any blank paper she encounters.

My Runaway Shadow